For Tyler & Naomi Keevil—
happy together!
M. D.

To Abigail, with love
C. U.

Text copyright © 2011 by Malachy Doyle
Illustrations copyright © 2011 by Caroline Uff

First published in Great Britain in June 2011 by Bloomsbury Publishing Plc.
Published in the United States of America in June 2011
by Walker Publishing Company, Inc., a division of Bloomsbury Publishing, Inc.
www.bloomsburykids.com

For information about permission to reproduce selections from this book, write to
Permissions, Walker BFYR, 175 Fifth Avenue, New York, New York 10010

Library of Congress Cataloging-in-Publication Data
Doyle, Malachy.
[Happy book]
Get happy / Malachy Doyle ; illustrated by Caroline Uff.
p.   cm.
ISBN 978-0-8027-2271-3
[1. Stories in rhyme. 2. Happiness—Fiction. 3. Behavior—Fiction.] I. Uff, Caroline, ill. II. Title.
PZ8.3.D756Get 2011   [E]—dc22   2010031000

Art created with mixed media
Typeset in Handy Sans

Printed in China by Toppan Leefung Printing, Ltd., Dongguan, Guangdong
1 3 5 7 9 10 8 6 4 2

GET HAPPY

Malachy Doyle

illustrated by Caroline Uff

Walker & Company  New York

Squabble less.

Share more!

Sniffle less.

Snuggle more!

GET
HAPPY

Grumble less.

Giggle more!

Zone out less.

Zoom around more!

Pick less.

Plant more!

Shout less.

Sing more!

Grab less.

Give more!

Tease less.

Tickle more!

Sulk less.

Sparkle more!

Worry less.

Wonder more!

Fearless for evermore!

Be strong!

Be happy!